I'LL PROTECT YOU FROM THE RAIN

Vinda K. Parker

Love and Hugs Publishing

©Copyright 2021

I'LL PROTECT YOU FROM THE RAIN

Vinda K Parker

First Printing 2021

Love and Hugs Publishing

Loveandhugspublishing@Outlook.com

So Much I Don't Understand

There are so many things I just don't understand, and you can probably say the same. Why would I need more cloud storage when I didn't even know I had it, and why would I pay for it? Why would six-year-olds prefer to watch another six-year-old play with toys on YouTube when they have the same toys at home? Why would a teenager rather converse on Snap-Chat with friends instead of talking face to face? How do people across the world know my home phone number, and what makes them think my computer is not working? Why in some states can a person walk in and purchase drugs that were illegal just a year ago and now buy those same drugs in every flavor and form? And why do I need an app on my phone to 'calm' me at the end of the day?

The list can go on and on. But there are some things I do understand – God and His plan for Salvation. You can find this amazingly simple and non-changing plan in the scriptures.

> **Luke 19:10** - *For the Son of man is come to seek and to save that which was lost.*

> **John 3:16** - *For God so loved the world, that he gave his only begotten Son, that whosoever believeth in him should not perish, but have everlasting life.*

> **Romans 10:9** - *That if thou shalt confess with thy mouth the Lord Jesus, and shalt believe in thine heart that God hath raised him from the dead, thou shalt be saved.*

> **Matthew 28:19** - *Go ye therefore, and teach all nations, baptizing them in the name of the Father, and of the Son, and of the Holy Ghost:*

So, in this world of confusion and chaos, there is one constant we can understand - **God and His love for His people.**

One Day at a Time

One day at a time sweet Jesus, that's all I'm asking of you,
Just give me the strength, to do every day, What I have to do.
Yesterday's gone, sweet Jesus. And tomorrow may never be
mine.
Lord, help me today, show me the way, One day at a time.

In 2013, my work put me on a long-term project traveling almost every week for 2½ years, and the above song by Patsy Cline became my mantra. Without God, the prayers of family and friends, I could not have made it through. It was tough, but we all have difficult times in our lives, times we cannot see how we can endure just one more day. But our focus cannot be on our problems or worrying about what next week, next month, or next year brings. Our focus must be on today, our relationship with God, how He has never left us, and how He holds tomorrow.

Hebrews 13:5C reads, *"I will never leave thee, nor forsake thee."* This verse is a promise that God delivers daily. But when faced with hard times, we forget. Then the words found in the model prayer read, *"Give us this day our daily bread,"* Matthew 6:11. Let's not look at this verse as God only providing food daily, but that He is ready to provide whatever we need if we ask in His name.

When we worry about tomorrow, we are not relying on God and His promise. We are trying to do God's work. God is leading us step by step, day by day; our job is to follow. Our faith should tell us that as God takes care of today, He will also care for tomorrow. So, Patsy had it right when she sang; tomorrow may never be mine. Lord, help me today, show me the way, One day at a time.

We Care

Have you ever thought about how many young people have no one that genuinely cares for them? No one to tell them of their importance and how much they are loved. No one to make sure they have what they need, whether spiritual, emotional, or physical? What if you stepped up and showed them you care?

Dictionary.com defines care as: to be concerned or solicitous; have thought or regard, to have a special preference, to make provision or look out for, to have an inclination, liking, fondness, or affection.

I Peter 5: 5-6 reads, *Humble yourselves therefore under the mighty hand of God, that he may exalt you in due time: Casting all your care upon him; for he careth for you.*

God cares for us; He proves it in His Word and the blessings He allows us to enjoy. We are good at saying what our young people need to do, but what do we need to do? Our responsibility is to show we care, not just to our children and grandchildren, but to **all** children.

Caring is one of the first steps in building a relationship with a child or with anyone. Let each of them know how much their accomplishments mean to you. Let them know their failures do not define them and how each stumble is a pathway to continue their journey to becoming successful adults.

Let them know we got your back,

we are here for you,

we love you

and WE CARE!

Shiny and New

Have you ever cleaned your gold or silver jewelry? You dip your bracelet or ring in the cleaning solution and then clean by rubbing with the cleaning cloth and polishing with the polishing cloths.

But as you polish, you notice the jewelry is not clean, you continue to rub and rub, and although it looks shiny and new, your cloth is getting dirtier and dirtier.

Does God feel that way about us? He polishes and rubs us in the direction of His love and understanding, and although we look shiny and new, we still need more work. Like our jewelry, we tarnish.

Tarnish is a chemical reaction when metal meets with a nonmetal element, usually oxygen or sulfur dioxide. However, we also get "tarnished" by being around and succumbing to non-God-like elements. But God is always there, ready to polish us if we would just ask.

Every tarnished piece of silver needs a good rub to get shinier. And what's on the polishing cloth? The carbonite (sin). The cloth is a little like Jesus, rubbing out our sins and taking them onto himself.

How can you become shiny and new? Let God be your polishing cloth!

■■■

Then Peter said, silver and gold have I none; but such as I have give I thee: In the name of Jesus Christ of Nazareth rise up and walk.

Acts 3:6

■■■

How to Eat an Elephant

Have you ever heard the riddle, 'how does an ant eat an elephant? Answer: One bite at a time. We sometimes refuse to move forward with what we need to do for fear of not accomplishing our goals. We believe we will bite off more than we can chew.

In our rush to do it all or have it all, we become discouraged, and life seems hard. We all have said, 'I need to read my Bible more, study more, pray more, lose weight, eat healthier… but it all seems too much. We just cannot get started.

But what if we followed the actions of the ant? What if we took one bite at a time? What if, instead of turning on the television each morning, we open our Bibles for just 10 minutes until it becomes part of our day and our time spent in the Word increases. What if, instead of that burger for lunch, we begin with a salad. What if, instead of taking that afternoon nap, we walked around the block. These actions are taking one bite at a time. This is how we eat an elephant.

God is so merciful in his Word; He knows our weaknesses, doubts, and fears. He even knows how small our faith is. Matthew 17:20 reads, *"If ye have faith as a grain of mustard seed, ye shall say unto this mountain, Remove hence to yonder place; and it shall remove; and nothing shall be impossible unto you."* This verse exemplifies us faithfully doing a little and God being faithful to do a lot.

So, the next time you think 'I just can't,' know that with God - you can. Just take it one bite at a time!

Evaluating Your Relationship

Have you ever evaluated your relationship with Christ? Do you ever think am I all that He wants me to be? We usually see the areas others are failing in their relationship but shy away from looking at our own. Starting today, earnestly seek God's guidance by asking:

- Where am I in my relationship with You, Lord?
- Where do You want me to be?
- How do I get there?

Answering the above questions is an excellent beginning to letting Christ live through us like never before.

Learn from yesterday,

live for today,

hope for tomorrow.

Albert Einstein

Christian Leadership

When we think of Christian leadership, we think of those who hold a church title - pastor, deacons, and other church staff. However, I once heard a quote that has stuck with me, 'You don't have to have a title to be a leader." This quote tells me we are all leaders, even those of us without an official title. The question is - what kind of leader are we?

To become the leader God wants us to be, we must first follow. Our prime example of a Christian leader is Jesus Christ. Therefore, we must know and believe who Jesus is. Matthew 6:33 reads, *But seek ye first the kingdom of God, and his righteousness; and all these things shall be added unto you.* Mark 16:16a reads, *He that believeth and is baptized shall be saved;*

Second, as leaders, we must know Jesus' mission on this earth. John 3:17 For God sent not his Son into the world to condemn the world; but that the world through him might be saved.

After understanding Jesus' mission, Matthew 28:19-20 tells what He left for us, His leaders to do, *Go ye therefore, and teach all nations, baptizing them in the name of the Father, and of the Son, and of the Holy Ghost: Teaching them to observe all things whatsoever I have commanded you: and, lo, I am with you always, even unto the end of the world. Amen.*

Third, as Christian leaders, we must be that example to others as Jesus' life is for us. II Timothy 2:22-24 (NIV) reads, *Flee the evil desires of youth and pursue righteousness, faith, love and peace, along with those who call on the Lord out of a pure heart. Don't have anything to do with foolish and stupid arguments, because you know they produce quarrels. And the Lord's servant must not be quarrelsome but must be kind to everyone, able to teach, not resentful.*

Christian Leadership (cont.)

Fourth as Christian leaders, we must prepare others to be leaders. Others walking beside us closes a considerable gap in our ministry. Satan's job is to increase his army, and without a strong Christian presence in your church, home, community, workplace, and schools, Satan's influence grows. Ephesians 6:10-12, *Finally, my brethren, be strong in the Lord, and in the power of his might. Put on the whole armour of God, that ye may be able to stand against the wiles of the devil. For we wrestle not against flesh and blood, but against principalities, against powers, against the rulers of the darkness of this world, against spiritual wickedness in high places.*

Christian Leadership takes on many forms. Ultimately it is about living our lives in a way that represents Christ. Are people turning to God because of how we live? Or are our actions and behaviors turning others away from God and the church? Believe me; we are doing one or the other.

Dear Father,

Enable me to live a life that does not turn people away from God but draws them near to Him.

Don't Be One of the Crazies

If you read your local newspaper, listened to the radio, or watched your favorite news channel, you probably found a week filled with sorrow, disaster, and craziness.

Do you ever think about how we can navigate the craziness of this world without becoming one of the crazies? How do we go day to day without being afraid to go anywhere - even church? How can we feel comfortable to fly or even drive without someone attacking us with road rage? And how do we remain faithful to what's right instead of taking the wrong or what we think is the easier path? One way is to turn to God's Word.

Fear not, for I am with you; be not dismayed, for I am your God; I will strengthen you, I will help you, I will uphold you with my righteous right hand. Isaiah 41:10 ESV

Do not be anxious about anything, but in everything by prayer and supplication with thanksgiving let your requests be made known to God. And the peace of God, which surpasses all understanding, will guard your hearts and your minds in Christ Jesus. Philippians 4:6-7 ESV

For God gave us a spirit not of fear but of power and love and self-control. 2 Timothy 1:7 ESV

I sought the LORD, and he answered me and delivered me from all my fears. Psalm 34:4 ESV

Just remember God is with you to sustain you during trying and stressful times. His love and understanding keep us from becoming one of the crazies.

Spiritual Maturity

After Salvation comes the expectation of spiritual growth that leads to *spiritual maturity*. Spiritual maturity is an ongoing process that never ends, and you achieve it by becoming more and more like Jesus Christ.

A mature Christian moves from pleasing self to pleasing and obeying God and has the characteristics found in Galatians 5:22-23a:

But the fruit of the Spirit is love, joy, peace, longsuffering, gentleness, goodness, faith, meekness, temperance:

If we grow in Christ, we see ourselves both loving God more and loving others more. When people see us, they should see someone in love with God and His people.

A mature Christian walks in the Spirit. To obtain spiritual maturity, we must be led by God's Holy Spirit and be in His control. Galatians 5:25 tells us:

If we live in the Spirit, let us also walk in the Spirit.

A spiritually mature person is effective and fruitful in the lives of others.

That the communication of thy faith may become effectual by the acknowledging of every good thing which is in you in Christ Jesus. Philemon 1:6

In our spiritual walk, we should be progressing toward maturity; we are either moving forward or backward. Which way are you moving?

Encourage Yourself

Sometimes you have to encourage yourself
Sometimes you have to speak victory during the test
And no matter how you feel
Speak the Word and you will be healed
Speak over yourself
Encourage yourself in the Lord

Some of you will recognize the above words as a song by Donald Lawrence and the Tri-City Singers. As a matter of fact, you may have found yourself singing it instead of reading it.

According to Merriam-Webster.com, encourage means to fill with courage or strength of purpose, the raising of one's confidence. If you are one of the lucky ones, you get encouragement from friends or family. I have what I call cheerleaders. My cheerleaders are those friends or family that, no matter what –are in my corner. They are there to encourage me, to give me confidence even when I do not quite have the nerve to take a much-needed step.

But what about those times when those cheerleaders are not around? What about those of you that do not have cheerleaders to encourage you? Those times are when we must look within and find the courage to move forward?

Romans 1:11-12 (NIV) reads, *I long to see you so that I may impart to you some spiritual gift to make you strong— that is, that you and I may be mutually encouraged by each other's faith.* In these verses, Paul longed to visit the people of Rome for many reasons; he longed to see them, to teach them, and because he knew he could be encouraged by these new Christians' faith. But until then, Paul had to encourage himself to do the work God had for him to do.

Encourage Yourself (cont.)

The downfall of not encouraging yourself or finding the encouragement of others is being discouraged. Discouragement is an act of Satan. That's why discouragement brings hopelessness, where encouragement brings hopefulness. Discouragement brings defeat, where encouragement brings victory. Discouragement brings death, where encouragement springs forward living.

Life creates uncertainty. Each life event should give us the courage to tackle the next one. Encourage yourself, say, God, you got me through last time, God you'll bring me through now. Encourage yourself, be your own cheerleader and share your experiences. That way, you not only encourage yourself, but you are an encouragement to others.

 **Go Me!!!**

Elevator Speech

Have you ever written an elevator speech? An elevator speech is a clear and brief message or commercial about an idea you are trying to communicate. An elevator speech lasts about 30 seconds, about the time it takes to ride from the bottom to the top in an elevator. An elevator speech prepares you to talk about a subject anytime to anyone – anywhere.

Now that leads to this question. What do you say to someone that approaches you as Nicodemus came to Jesus and said, "How can a man be born when he is old?" Or as the keeper of the prison asked Paul and Silas, Sirs, what must I do to be saved? Are you prepared to answer those questions?

What if someone comes to you in need because of their life's circumstances? Think about it, what would you say? Do you have a scripture you can quote and offer? Do you have a personal testimony you can share?

God does give us what we need when we need it. He does bring things back to our remembrance, but look at it this way, He cannot bring something back that we never had.

So, if you are not prepared to talk to someone in need, prepare yourself today; someone may need to hear from God - through you - tomorrow.

■■

Then he called for a light, and sprang in, and came trembling, and fell down before Paul and Silas, and brought them out, and said, Sirs, what must I do to be saved?

Acts 16:29-30
■■

It was Good

Each year spring turns into summer. All the signs are there; we are cutting our grass once or twice a week, our once dormant flowers are in full bloom, and our days involve many trips to Wal-Mart and Lowes' Garden Centers for everything we need to increase the beauty of our lawns.

We look out and stand proud of how our now beautifully manicured lawns reflect our hard work and style. But after just a few days, it seems what we worked hard to do was in vain, the grass has grown two inches, and the weeds and dandelions are back.

Have you ever thought about what God thinks when He looks out at His work? Genesis 1 reads. *'In the beginning God created the heaven and the earth.'* That same book tells us how He spoke light, vegetation, animals, birds, fish, and man and woman into existence. Genesis 1:25C says, *'and God saw that it was good.'*

God also looks out and sees the weeds and dandelions in His garden. Could those weeds be man? Yes, those weeds are us, you and me.

Just a few chapters later (Genesis 6:12) reads, *'And God looked upon the earth, and behold, it was corrupt; for all flesh had corrupted his way upon the earth.'*

Instead of being like us, plucking the weeds, and investing in weed killer, God demonstrates His love and sent His Son to save us from our sin.

So, the next time you look out on your lawn and smile, think of God looking down on you, consider what can I do to make God smile and say **it was good?**

Things We Should Teach Our Children

Train up a child in the way he should go: and when he is old, he will not depart from it. Proverbs 22:6

Many of us have heard this verse, and most of us can recite it by heart, but how many of us have thought of it when it comes to training our children how to be better stewards of their finances?

The first step in teaching our children about budgeting and finances is by being an example of what God expects. *"Bring ye all the tithes into the storehouse, that there may be meat in mine house, and prove me now herewith, saith the LORD of hosts, if I will not open you the windows of heaven, and pour you out a blessing, that there shall not be room enough to receive it."* Malachi 3:10. Do you let your children know why you contribute to the church and what method you use to determine the amount you give? God wants our first fruits, not what we may have left this week, and our children need to know why we live by this principle.

Many of us never set an allowance for our children; we give them money when they want or need something. But what if we budget each month how much we can afford to give our children? And what if we taught them how to save for their wants and needs. These steps can teach them you are not an unlimited supply of cash and that what they buy lands on them and not you.

So, if they spend their money on candy and don't have any money left when their friends head to the movies – they will learn to save their money and be more responsible.

Things We Should Teach Our Children (cont.)

We must teach our children to be satisfied with what God has blessed us with, that contentment does not come from what we have but with our relationship with God. *"Not that I speak in respect of want: for I have learned, in whatsoever state I am, therewith to be content."* Philippians 4:11.

Matthew 6:25 reads, *"Therefore I say unto you, Take no thought for your life, what ye shall eat, or what ye shall drink; nor yet for your body, what ye shall put on. Is not the life more than meat, and the body than raiment?"* And then we are told why we do not have to worry, *"But seek ye first the kingdom of God, and his righteousness; and all these things shall be added unto you."* Matthew 6:33.

These are things we should teach our children.

■■

But Jesus called the children to him and said, "Let the little children come to me, and do not hinder them, for the kingdom of God belongs to such as these. Truly I tell you, anyone who will not receive the kingdom of God like a little child will never enter it."

Luke 18:16-17 (NIV)

■■

Be an Influencer of Others

Control. We all want to think we have everything under control; we control what goes on around us and have total control over what happens. But do we? Do you realize we control very little? We can control ourselves (through God's Holy Spirit), but we have very little control over others and what they do.

But what we do have is influence. According to Bing.com, Influence is the capability to affect the character, development, or behavior of someone or something.

1 Timothy 4:12 reads, *"Let no man despise thy youth; but be thou an example of the believers, in word, in conversation, in charity, in Spirit,*

Don't you know you are not just a member of your church or community? You are an example for others to follow. You may think, 'But who is following me?' You may not realize it, but someone wants to be just like you, but are you a good example – are you a Godly influence for others?

Before we can influence others toward godliness, we must be under God's influence—seeking God's direction, obeying Him, and being where we're supposed to be so God can use us.

Consider these verses when thinking about the influence you can have on others,

"Let no corrupt communication proceed out of your mouth, but that which is good to the use of edifying, that it may minister grace unto the hearers." Ephesians 4:29

Be an Influencer of Others (cont.)

"Only let your conversation be as it becometh the gospel of Christ: that whether I come and see you, or else be absent, I may hear of your affairs, that ye stand fast in one spirit, with one mind striving together for the faith of the gospel;" Philippians 1:27

"Finally, brethren, whatsoever things are true, whatsoever things are honest, whatsoever things are just, whatsoever things are pure, whatsoever things are lovely, whatsoever things are of good report; if there be any virtue, and if there be any praise, think on these things." Philippians 4:8

Whether you believe it or not, you are an influencer of others; it's your decision if your example edifies Christ or one that pleases Satan.

As An Act of Love

Greater love hath no man than this, that a man lay down his life for his friends. John 15:13

In a review of the scriptures, the word love appears hundreds of times; however, John 3:16 demonstrates the most sacrificial act of love. *For God so loved the world, that he gave his only begotten Son, that whosoever believeth in him should not perish, but have everlasting life.* Just one example of God's love for us.

God also commands us to love Him. Matthew 22:37 Jesus said unto him, *Thou shalt love the Lord thy God with all thy heart, and with all thy soul, and with all thy mind.*

After our love for Him, we are to love one another. *For this is the message that ye heard from the beginning, that we should love one another* 1 John 3:11 and Romans 12:10 reads *Be kindly affectioned one to another with brotherly love; in honour preferring one another.*

Several scriptures in the Bible teach us to love our neighbors as thyself. That tells us that the love that comes from God is unselfish, a love where the needs of others are equal to our own needs.

There are many ways to express our love for God and his people. Can't think of any? Seek God's guidance. And follow Jesus' many many acts of His unselfish love?

God Listens to You

Has anyone ever said to you, "You don't listen" or "Could you just listen for five minutes?" Most or possibly all of us have heard something similar to that. It seems listening is a big problem for us, and it can lead to miscommunication.

Although listening may not be our best attribute, it is one of God's. **"The Lord sees the good people and listens to their prayers" (1 Peter 3:12).**

God wants you to keep looking for him by praying, reading his Word, and living out your faith. *"Come and pray to me, and I will listen to you,"* God says. *"You will seek me and find me when you seek me with all your heart"* (Jeremiah 29:12-13, NIV).

Do you sometimes say, I feel far from God right now? I pray and hear nothing. How do I know he's listening? Or even there? I'm afraid I'm missing his answers or that he's not hearing me.

You're not alone. Almost every Christian feels this way sometimes. Read Psalm 22:1-2. King David, who certainly knew God, wrote: *"My God, my God, why have you forsaken me? ... I cry out by day, but you do not answer"* (NIV). We often feel God is distant or disconnected. Even Jesus felt this way—and quoted this Psalm—when he was on the cross.

Because God understands our doubts and fears, Scripture is full of examples testifying that he hears us. Psalms provides multiple affirmations of this truth. Psalm 4:3 says, *"The Lord hears when I call to him"* (NIV). Psalm 5:3 tells us, *"Lord, you hear my voice"* (NIV). Psalm 6:8 reassures us that *"the Lord has heard my weeping."* **In prayer, God hears more than your words— He listens to your heart.**

Relax, Close Your Eyes, and Go to Sleep

When traveling for work, I usually returned home on Thursday, but this one particular week, I came home on Friday night. Friday and night are two things I tried to avoid when it came to business travel, but this week both were necessary. When I first stepped onto the plane, I noticed it was hot. I don't mean a little warm – I mean hot. The air conditioner that cooled the aircraft while on the ground was not working, and it was miserable with the 100° day I was leaving.

My next issue was that the woman in seat 11B sitting beside me decided to bathe in her perfume, which was not a good combination with the heat. Then I found out she was in the wrong seat, she actually was supposed to be in 9B, but that person was 'kind' enough to let her stay where she was. Next, someone onboard decides to eat their dinner; it smelled like a combination of body odor and onion. Then, of course, there were the two guys that had the heated discussion about overhead space and the one 'bad word' person taking up room with a small backpack where a suitcase should go. Since I was still on the ground watching the boarding process, I texted Michael all the misadventures I was experiencing. Although he felt sorry for me, he thought it was hilarious. However, he followed with a text saying, *'relax, close your eyes and go to sleep.'*

And that I did. When I woke up, I was in the air, the air conditioner was cooling, and with air now circulating the odors from Perfume Lady and Onion Man, the flight was bearable.

The moral of the story: the discomfort I was feeling was too small and insignificant to take to God. But each of us has situations that only God can solve, money issues, divorce, sickness, death, work problems. These problems take the love and understanding that only God can provide. Matthew 11:28 reads, *"Come unto me, all ye that labour and are heavy laden, and I will give you rest."* In other words, He is saying, *'I got this, relax, close your eyes, and go to sleep. '*

"Reach high, for stars lie hidden in your soul. Dream deep, for every dream precedes the goal."

Pamela Vaull Starr

I'll Protect You from the Rain

Recently I saw a video of a small boy whose family had warned him of the arrival of an impending hurricane. As he stood holding an umbrella larger than him, he looked up at his mother and said, "Momma, I'll protect you from the rain."

This young boy made me reflect on our relationship with God and His umbrella of protection.   How often have we left our umbrella home and a rainstorm hit, or in the car when we just ran into the store for a minute? The wonderful thing about God being our umbrella of protection is no matter what storms come our way or when they come our way; He is there to keep us safe from danger. Hebrews 13:5C reassures us of God's protecting power, *"for he hath said, I will never leave thee, nor forsake thee."*

However, we must believe, like the Psalmist in 91:2, *"I will say of the Lord, He is my refuge and my fortress; my God; in him will I trust."* And verse 3 follows with, *"Surely he shall deliver thee from the snare of the fowler, and from the noisome pestilence."*

But it seems we still leave our umbrella of protection at home or our car, instead of in our hearts. God has said to each of us, "I'll protect you from the rain." Our job is to constantly pray and thank God for His safety and peace.

Our job is to trust and believe he will do what He said He would do!!

Rise, Take Up Thy Bed and Walk!

*"And a certain man was there, which had an infirmity thirty and eight years. When Jesus saw him lie, and knew that he had been now a long time in that case, he saith unto him, Wilt thou be made whole? The impotent man answered him, Sir, I have no man, when the water is troubled, to put me into the pool: but while I am coming, another steppeth down before me. Jesus saith unto him, **Rise, take up thy bed, and walk.** And immediately the man was made whole, and took up his bed, and walked:"*
John 5: 5-9a

When I read this, I think of how it applies to our lives. This Scripture tells of a man with a disease, a disease that was holding him back, of a man that was full of excuses that were holding him back, but he was a man that had a desire to be healed, he was a man that knew where to go to be healed.

How many of us identify with the man with the disease? We are paralyzed with our problems, fears, and financial difficulties and have excuses for why we cannot move forward. Like the man with the crippling disease, we are holding ourselves back. We know where to go to be healed, but we focus on our situation instead of turning to God. We forget God is faithful to His Word. II Chronicles 20:15b tells us, *"Thus saith the LORD unto you, Be not afraid nor dismayed by reason of this great multitude; for the battle is not yours, but God's."* Isaiah 41:10 reads, *"Fear thou not; for I am with thee: be not dismayed; for I am thy God: I will strengthen thee; yea, I will help thee; yea, I will uphold thee with the right hand of my righteousness."*

Instead of letting worry and stress keep you in your current situations, rely on your faith and trust in our Lord and Savior; He is telling each of us, as He did with the man with the crippling disease, **Rise, take up thy bed and walk!**

24

Burden Bearing
It Doesn't Have to Cost You a Dime

Bear ye one another's burdens, and so fulfil the law of Christ.
Galatians 6:2

We must make a deliberate choice to do what is in our power to ease the pain of others or to lend support when needed.

You may say, "but I'm broke, my pockets are empty, I can barely help myself." There are always ways to impact the lives of others - but we must make burden bearing a priority in our lives.

There are some things we can do that does not cost us a dime:

Prayer: Recently, I saw a group of 4-5 people in a circle of prayer in Lowes. You will never know how this one act of kindness can impact the person in need.

Listen: Sometimes, people just need to talk, and we can be there to listen. Not give a solution, just be someone to listen to what is paining others.

Time: 24 hours is given to each of us every day. What if you gave someone a couple of hours of your 24 to help them when needed?

Talent: God gives us all talents, be creative, and find ways to use that skill to help others.

You may not have money to help others. Galatians 6:2 commands us to be burden bearers; it's our job to find ways to do so. However, if burden-bearing does take your last dime, God has many, many more to replace it.

Philippians 4:19 - *And my God shall supply all your need according to His riches in glory by Christ Jesus.*

Tell Your Story

A true witness delivereth souls:
Proverbs 14:25A

Do you know someone that can tell a great story? A story that captures your attention, a story that you remembered even days, weeks, and maybe even years later. A story that helped you learn much-needed information. We all have stories to tell; we just need to tell them.

Most will say I am not a great storyteller, or I have nothing important going on in my life to tell. But we all have stories that can help others. The world is looking for answers, and we have solutions in our many life experiences. Many of us have lost our parents, lost a child, lost our wife or husband. As an act of love, think of how your story can help someone going through similar situations. What about those who have gone through sickness, GOD, recovered from drug or alcohol abuse, GOD, lost our jobs, GOD, divorce, GOD. Maybe you woke up one morning with a terrible headache or a twinge in your back, and you still were able to work your total eight hours, GOD. Did you have a bill due or past due, and the money unexpectedly came through? GOD.

Our most important story to tell is the story of our Salvation. How God saved our soul, and how God can save the soul of others.

No matter what your situation, give God the glory and share your story.

'Ye are my witnesses, saith the LORD, and my servant whom I have chosen: that ye may know and believe me, and understand that I am he: before me there was no God formed, neither shall there be after me. I, even I, am the LORD; and beside me there is no saviour.' Isaiah 43:10-11

You Are Not Your Label

Have you ever been shopping, tried on that pair of slacks or that beautiful dress, looked at the label, and could not believe it did not fit? The label contained your size, but clearly, it was not **your** label, so you refused to move up to the next size and left the store.

Other than dress labels, we label ourselves or allow others to label us. Short, tall, fat, skinny, blonde, red-headed, intelligent, stupid, and with all labels come stereotypes. Fat means you are unhealthy; however, we also think skinny means you're unhealthy, red-headed means you are high tempered, tall means you are athletic and short means you are not. But don't accept it, don't let a label define who you are. Only you determine who you are!

However, there is one label we should all accept and be proud of. The label of Christianity, being Christ-like. Galatians 6:22-23 labels the character of a Christian as fruit - love, joy, peace, longsuffering, gentleness, goodness, faith, meekness, and temperance. These labels define a Christian, so the next time you try on that pair of slacks that are just too snug, look at the label; if it does not say 'Christian' or 'Child of God', move on to the next size, because you are not your label!

Small

Medium,

Large

Christian!!!

27

How to Prepare a Potato

Have you ever thought about how many ways you can prepare a potato? You can fry, bake, boil, stuff, roast, season, mash, parsley, butter, and if you are a real potato lover, you are pleased with each and every way. You just pick which way you want them prepared and eat them for breakfast, lunch, and dinner.

Some people feel worshipping God is like preparing potatoes; you pick what you want and serve it up. Worship is not a smorgasbord. God is not pleased with every way as we are with potatoes. He has one way of worship and lets us know in John 4. John 4:23 tells us God is seeking true worshippers that worship Him in Spirit and truth. Verse 24 follows and says, 'they that worship him **MUST** worship him in spirit and in truth.' This verse is not a suggestion or recommendation but a command.

So, the next time you bend your knees in thanksgiving or raise your hands in praise, make sure you are worshipping to please God and not serving it up as you would your next plate of potatoes.

■■■

God is a Spirit: and they that worship him must worship him in Spirit and in truth.

John 4:24
■■■

Start – Stop – Continue

Many organizations use a change management tool called Start – Stop – Continue. This exercise is an easy way to identify behaviors/actions that should stop or start and behaviors/actions that should continue.

What if we used this same tool to identify and help us find those things in our lives that **we** need to start, stop, and continue?

Start – What are those things in my life that I am not doing, and I need to start? Examples...

- A regular prayer and study time

- Visiting and caring for someone in need

- An exercise routine and eating healthier

Stop – What are those things in my life that I am doing that God is not pleased with that I need to stop? Examples...

- Acts of hate and envy

- Gossiping

- My addictions – social media, smoking,...

Continue – What are those things in my life that are pleasing to God that I need to continue? Examples...

- Regularly attending worship services

- Expressing love and concern for others

- Reading my Bible

So today, take an assessment of your life. What are those things that please God? What things hinder us from living up to our potential and expectations of our relationship with our Lord and Savior, Jesus Christ? Then, Start - Stop - Continue.

The Black Church

It is almost impossible to discuss our childhood experiences without discussing the impact of the black church on our lives. Anyone over the age of 35 knows church was a significant part of their childhood. As children, if you met a new friend, you asked their name and then asked, 'what church do you go to?' If you wanted to visit a friend, your parents had to know their folks, and if they were not a 'church-going' family, you could not go to their house.

The black church was a place we came to worship, a place of fellowship. It was a place we learned to get through difficult times and where we knew we could find encouragement.

The Black church was not only for church services but also a place of community and family. For many of us, the church was our only 'social' life; we looked forward to being with friends at church. Most of our great African American leaders and musicians got their start in the church. During the civil rights era, ministers and teachers used the church to deliver their messages.

Most of us can testify that our best life lessons came from the church, and the black church was where our talents and courage were first cultivated. If you were down or sick, the black church showed up with whatever they had to help you through.

So, as the church evolves into modern-day, let's not forget the black church and its impact on us all.

As for Me and My House...

but as for me and my house, we will serve the LORD.
Joshua 24:15D

Each day, we must make choices, what time to get up, where to go, what to eat. Choices. In Joshua 24:15, Joshua made a bold choice for him and his family, *"but as for me and my house, we will serve the LORD."* As head of the household, he took a stance that his family would be of the household of faith. His concern was not only for himself and his family, but he found it his responsibility to leave the people of Israel in the hands of the Lord. But he knew it had to be their choice.

Joshua 24 is about making choices based on sound information. We, too, are forced to make choices on how to lead our family. Should we attend church services or not, should we vote, and if we do, who to vote for, vaccine/no vaccine, what to let our children do during their free time. And where do we get that information to make those informed decisions? Some from the local and national newspapers, some CNN, some watch Fox, and some chose Facebook and other social media sites. But as Christians, we realize the right choices come by spending time with the Lord.

God hears and answers prayers.   Just like parents wait to hear from their children, God is waiting to communicate with you. He is the one to discuss your concerns, and He is the one to guide you in the right direction to every choice you need to make.

So, like Joshua, make a choice, and make that choice based on sound information gathered while communicating in prayer with our Lord and Savior!!

212 Degrees

At 211 degrees...water is hot.
At 212 degrees...it boils.
And with boiling water, comes steam.
And steam can power a locomotive.
And, its that one extra degree that...
Makes all the difference.

Taken from *212° the extra degree* by Sam Parker

Have you ever thought, 'I cannot push myself any further; I cannot go just one more degree?   Could you be giving up too quickly? Are you letting Satan remove your power, inserting doubt in your mind, and are you becoming less and less of who God wants you to be? When God offers courage and Satan offers fear, are you choosing fear because it seems easier?

According to George Patton, American soldier and general, Courage is fear holding on a minute longer.

Thomas Edison said Many of life's failures are men who did not realize how close they were to success when they gave up.

Galatians 6:9NIV reads *Let us not become weary in doing good, for at the proper time we will reap a harvest if we do not give up.*

So, look at it this way, with a little extra effort and faith in God's plan, you could change your life, someone else's life, or even the world!

A Pencil for Ten Dollars

When our sons were small, we sent a dollar bill each day with them for lunch. One morning around 8:30 AM, I received a call from Brian's teacher asking did I know Brian had brought ten dollars to school? In checking my wallet, I realized that morning; in my hurry, I had given him a ten-dollar bill instead of the usual one dollar. I simply told the teacher just to let him buy his lunch and send the change home. Well, this was not as simple as I thought; he had already used the ten-dollar bill to buy a pencil. Not a special pencil, or one that was worth ten dollars, but a plain pencil! However, the teacher was able to reverse the transaction and send my change home.

Don't we do that, but on a larger scale? I would love to ask him, why did our 6-year-old Brian think it reasonable to purchase a pencil for ten dollars? Why do we – just because God blesses us with a little extra - believe we need to use it on something we don't need? Why do we take what God has blessed us with, whether it's money, time, or talent, and not ask Him how we should use it?

God expects us to be responsible stewards of His blessings. I Peter 4:10 reads, *Each of you should use whatever gift you have received to serve others, as faithful stewards of God's grace in its various forms.* So, when God blesses you, what will you do with your blessing? Will you buy a pencil for $10, or will you use it to glorify God?

Should We Pray for Revival?

One or two times a year, most churches conduct revival services. Does that mean you only need revival during those traditional times of the year? I say no. Revival is personal, and only you know when you need revival.

We sometimes look at revival as a time to bring the lost to Christ. But REVIVAL is not about evangelism (although this is our job), but revival is what God sends, not to the lost, but to His people, the church. However, if we do as God leads us, evangelism flows out of revival.

What is revival? Bing.com defines revival as an improvement in the condition or strength of something, a reawakening of religious fervor, especially by means of a series of evangelistic meetings, a restoration to bodily or mental vigor, to life or consciousness.

When is revival needed among God's people? When we have left our first love. We need revival when we find ourselves going through the motions, having "a form of godliness but denying its power" (2nd Timothy 3:5). We need revival when we are wallowing in sin but unwilling to thoroughly repent of that sin. We need revival when we are neglecting our relationship with Christ.

Is there a "formula for revival"? One Scripture, 2nd Chronicles 7:14, can be used as a formula for revival:

"If My people who are called by My name will humble themselves, and pray and seek My face, and turn from their wicked ways, then I will hear from heaven, and will forgive their sin and heal their land."

So, should we pray for revival? Of course! Revival is the work of God. We pray for it because we are dependent upon Him to send it.

Moral Compass

Have you ever been called a moral compass, or do you know someone that you consider one? Or do you even know what a moral compass is? Think of a regular compass. It has north, south, east, and west, and no matter which direction you head in, it lets you know which way you are going. If you need to go north, and the compass shows you heading south, the compass silently points south, and you can see where north is. Now, it is up to you to go the right way. You may say, 'Oh, you mean a GPS?' But no, a GPS does tell you when you go wrong, but it also tells you turn by turn how to go the right way. A compass does not tell you turn by turn; it just silently lets you know you are headed wrong and shows you what right looks like.

That is what a moral compass does for you. A moral compass is that person that helps us define what kind of behavior is right or wrong behavior just by their presence.

How can you know if you are a moral compass? When you walk in a room, and everyone is laughing, do they suddenly stop, when someone curses, do they look at you and apologize? Then you are a moral compass.

Without a moral compass, some people will make decisions or exhibit un-Christ-like behaviors without thinking through the consequences of their actions. The Holy Spirit leads and guides us, but we also influence the behavior of others. We need to be moral examples to our friends, relatives, co-workers, and church members. Someone that helps others see right when they are wrong. It does not mean as a moral compass, you are perfect and never make a mistake, but that you have a set of values that help guide others to the ways of the Lord. Therefore, be that example, be that person others admire and emulate. Be their **Moral Compass**. *In all thy ways acknowledge him, and he shall direct thy paths.* Proverbs 3:6

But on God's Time

Have you ever put together a puzzle, and when you finished the puzzle, you found one, two, and maybe even three pieces were missing? You now think your puzzle will never be the picture-perfect design on the box, so in frustration, you threw the puzzle away. Then later, you find the missing pieces under the sofa or bed.

Isn't life like that? You see your picture-perfect life ahead, but it seems the pieces just will not fall into place. You pray for God's blessings on your situation, and you don't find the answers. You wait for days and maybe weeks and then become frustrated and throw it all away, just like you threw away your puzzle.

God has your missing pieces; however, you must live a God-focused life, be patient, and wait for God to reveal them. Just like you found your missing puzzle pieces, you will discover God's plan for your life. Psalms 27:14 reads, *"Wait on the LORD: be of good courage, and he shall strengthen thine heart: wait, I say, on the LORD."*

When we wait on the Lord, we find all the pieces fall into place, maybe not on our time, but on God's time.

We believe in God,

But more importantly,

HE believes in us!

Trust Me

Has anyone ever said to you – "Trust me," "Trust me, I wouldn't steer you wrong," or "Trust me, I know how you feel"? We trust them, follow their advice, and cannot understand why our situation did not come out as we hoped.

We must KNOW if God sent the person who came to us with their trust and if they are worthy to be trusted with our secrets, lives, spiritual experiences, and family situations.

Trust is an essential aspect of our relationship with others, but it is more critical to our relationship with God.

Psalm 118:8 reads, *It is better to trust in the LORD than to put confidence in man.* Does this mean we should not trust others? Of course not, but we must be cautious who we trust and look to God for guidance in all situations. In other words, we must begin by trusting God first. Psalm 118:6 reads *The LORD is on my side; I will not fear: what can man do unto me?* This verse tells us if others do fail us, God is there to lift us back up.

Proverbs 3:5-6 reads, *Trust in the LORD with all thine heart; and lean not unto thine own understanding. In all thy ways acknowledge him, and he shall direct thy paths.*

So, the next time someone says – "Trust ME, just make sure you are trusting God first!

Are You A Social Influencer?

Some of you may ask, what is a social influencer? An influencer is an individual on social media who has the power to affect the decisions of others because of their knowledge, position, or relationship with their audience. Some influencers have an audience of more than a million followers and can make upwards of $250,000 for each post they make on a topic.

What if we all decided to become influencers? But instead of marketing lipstick and the latest technology for money, we talked to others about God and how following Him can profoundly change their lives? What if we used our experiences with our Lord and Savior to let others know God hears and answers prayers and that He is a Savior to those that believe? What if we read to them John 3:16 and Romans 10 or gave them those scriptures to read themselves? What if we invited them to Sunday School and morning worship?

As Christians, we should use our knowledge and relationship with God to influence those we meet and not let them get their influence from social media.

Thankfulness and Gratitude to Him

How endearing it is for your three or four-year-old to ask for a piece of candy or glass of milk and, upon receiving it, looks up with wide-eyed wonder, smiles, and says thank you. It makes us want to do more to see them say it again and again. This act shows they are learning the rules of thankfulness and gratitude we taught them.

But are we practicing what we preach? How often have we asked God for safety, protection, needs, wants, etc., and after receiving God's blessing, we failed to say, 'Thank You, God!' We continue to enjoy the benefits of His love but never express the gratitude He deserves.

When our children refuse to say thank you – we refuse to grant their request. Let's be thankful God is not like us. He is a God of love and continues His blessings despite our shortfalls.

Romans 1:21-22 (NKJV) lets us know the consequences if we forget who He is and if we are not grateful and thankful. *Because, although they knew God, they did not glorify Him as God, nor were thankful, but became futile in their thoughts, and their foolish hearts were darkened. Professing to be wise, they became fools.*

Being thankful opens the door for continued blessings; it brings us closer to God. Just like we love to give gifts of love to our grateful children, God loves to bless us that show thankfulness and gratitude to HIM.

■■

Piglet noticed that even though he had a very small heart, it could hold a rather large amount of gratitude.
A A Milne, Writer, Playwright, Author, Creator of the Winnie the Pooh series
■■

A Dream Come True

Black History Month is an annual celebration of achievements by African Americans and a time for recognizing the central role of blacks in U.S. history. When we think of those to celebrate, we think of Dr. King, President Barack Obama, Willie Mays, Shirley Chisholm... Men and women that had a dream and lived out that dream.

Have you ever thought about your dreams and whether those dreams make your community, nation, church, or home better for others? It's not just those leaders that God gave a dream, we all have dreams, but we must deliberately find ways to act on those dreams. How many of us have had a dream and let ourselves or others talk us out of that dream? Most dreams are simply God's plan for our lives, and we let His plan slip by us. Our fear and diminished faith keep us from executing God's Plan.

God has dreams for us that are much bigger than any plan we can have for ourselves. So, what are your dreams? Pray, search the scriptures, and find ways to make your dreams come true.

As for these four children, God gave them knowledge and skill in all learning and wisdom: and Daniel had understanding in all visions and dreams.

Daniel 1:17

JACKSON!!!

Let me tell you about Jackson. No, I don't 'really' know him, but on a recent trip to Piggly Wiggly, he was there. How do I know his name? I heard it constantly while on that quick run into the store. Jackson was into everything, and his parents were, 'Jackson, STOP, Jackson, don't do that! Jackson, leave that alone. And then Jackson started running, and you guessed it – his mother started chasing him all over the store. In other words, *Jackson was running amuck.*

For some odd reason, this uncontrolled scene made me think of our Heavenly Father and us. Does He think of us as running amuck? Does He shake His head, as I did with Jackson, when we refuse to follow His plan for our lives, and we follow the ways of the evil one? What about our lying, cheating, excessive drinking, drugs, child abuse, molestation, racism, killing, stealing, gossiping, cursing, and any thoughts or actions not guided by our Lord?

Above are acts of the flesh; you can find others in Galatians 5:19. Verse 21 tells us that those that live this way will not inherit the kingdom of God. However, Galatians 5 not only tell us how not to live but describes the characteristics of how we should live. *'But the fruit of the Spirit is love, joy, peace, longsuffering, gentleness, goodness, faith, Meekness, temperance: against such there is no law.'* v 22-23.

When you look at your life and realize you are running amuck, turn to God's Word. God and His Word can turn your life into a life of peace and joy.

Are You a Fruit Bearer?

And he spake many things unto them in parables, saying, Behold, a sower went forth to sow; (Matthew 13:3) And when he sowed, some seeds fell by the way side, (Matthew 13:4a) *Some fell upon stony places,* (Matthew 13:5a) *But other fell into good ground, and brought forth fruit, some an hundredfold, some sixtyfold, some thirtyfold.* (Matthew 13:8)

As we all know, a healthy plant produces fruit. However, in the context above, the word *fruit* is produced in us by God's Holy Spirit.

Jesus clearly tells us what we must do to bear good fruit. He said, *Abide in me, and I in you. As the branch cannot bear fruit of itself, except it abide in the vine; no more can ye, except ye abide in me. I am the vine, ye are the branches: He that abideth in me, and I in him, the same bringeth forth much fruit: for without me ye can do nothing.* (John 15:4–5) When we neglect our spiritual life, ignore the Word of God, skimp on prayer, and withhold areas of our lives from God, we are like a branch broken off the vine. A broken branch quickly dies and withers away.

According to Galatians 5, we can bear two types of fruit: lust of the flesh and Fruit of the Spirit. For those that follow the flesh, Galatians 5:21c says *that they which do such things shall not inherit the kingdom of God.* However, Jesus told His followers (those bearing the Fruit of the Spirit), *Ye have not chosen me, but I have chosen you, and ordained you, that ye should go and bring forth fruit, and that your fruit should remain: that whatsoever ye shall ask of the Father in my name, he may give it you.* (John 15:16).

Be Still and Know That I am God!

Psalm 46 contains the above title. Verse 10 reads, *Be still, and know that I am God: I will be exalted among the heathen, I will be exalted in the earth.* However, the previous verses explain the true meaning of verse 10; they proclaim God's power and how we can find security in his care. When we are still and surrendered to God, we find peace even when it seems our world is falling apart, or our life is in chaos.

When circumstances are overwhelming, read Psalm 46:1, *"God is our refuge and strength, an ever-present help in trouble."* Be thankful God is always there. Run to Him, lay at His feet, and fall into His arms.

Don't let circumstances intimidate you. God is a God of love. Use this time to turn from your situation and focus on Him. Verse 9 tells us that *He maketh wars to cease unto the end of the earth; he breaketh the bow, and cutteth the spear in sunder; he burneth the chariot in the fire.* In other words, God is there to fight our battles, be still, and know that He is God.

Be Still, and Know that I Am God.

Psalm 46:10A

In the Words of a Child

"You need to ask for a day off so you can go to church." Those are the words of Peyton, our precocious seven-year-old friend to a cashier at Kroger. Although a bold statement for a seven-year-old, it needed to be said. But why did it take a child to say it?

We can look at this situation in two ways. One. Why is a seven-year-old doing what we should be doing, and two, why do we find every reason under the sun not to attend services at church?

It's all our responsibility to invite those we meet to church, share the plan of Salvation, and share our testimony of how serving and living for God has blessed our lives. We are responsible for holding others accountable for their actions, but our boldness disappears when God places us in situations to speak for Him. He is a God of courage and gives it to all that asks. If He puts someone in our path, He has made way for us to do His will.

Then, after speaking to someone about the plan of Salvation, we hear 'I can't go to church because I have to work, I don't have the right clothes, Sunday is when I get my rest or clean my house, I need to get my life together first, or the best one ever, they ain't right out there.' Well, in a way, we are not right, not yet anyway. However, we serve a God that can get us and them right, and attending services and learning more of what He has for our lives is how we get right. Hebrews 10:25 tells us not to forsake assembling ourselves together. The church is where God reveals His message for our lives, where we come to encourage each other, and where we establish lasting relationships.

The next time God presents someone to you that needs an encouraging word, be the example to that eager to learn seven-year-old, invite that person to church and hold them accountable for their actions.

Things Aren't What They Used to Be

Have you ever heard someone say, 'things aren't what they used to be'? In some cases, this is a good thing, but when it comes to the spiritual enlightenment of our children, it's not. I remember going to church as the highlight of our week, and everyone we knew and loved went to church somewhere. People filled the church buildings to compacity, and you could feel the power of God's Spirit as it rang out from all corners. We talked about God and church in our homes and even spent time playing bible games.

Our children today do not have those same experiences. Most of their friends are not in church, could not recite a bible verse if asked, and the saddest thing is, they have not accepted God as their Lord and Savior.

Dawson McAlister, a national youth ministry specialist, in his book "Building Faith at Home," stated another disturbing aspect. "90% of kids active in high school church youth groups do not go to church by the time they are sophomores in college." 1/3 will never return. How many of our families have children, grandchildren, nieces, nephews, or friends who have turned their backs on God and His church?

So, what can we do to bring our children back to the ways of Christianity and the church? It must be intentional. It must be a priority in our lives to pass on what we believe and what we hold essential to our children. We must bring back praying and singing songs of praise in front of our children, we must add bible readings and studies to their daily routine, we must talk about God and His power, and we must be friends and make sure their friends have the same values and beliefs we hold sacred.

So, the next time you think, 'things aren't what they used to be,' make sure it's not our children and their relationship with God.

Now That's Good News!

According to a recent survey by the American Psychological Association, when it comes to the daily news, more than half of those surveyed said the information causes them stress, and many report anxiety, fatigue, or loss of sleep as a result. Despite the heartburn caused by the news, one in ten adults checks the news every hour, and 20% report constantly monitoring their social media feeds, which often exposes them to the latest headlines, whether they want to see them or not.

In all this world of craziness and bad news, do you realize we need good news? Proverbs 15:30 (NASB) reads *Bright eyes gladden the heart; Good news puts fat on the bones.*

But where can we find good news? Our Scriptures are full of good news – news we will not find on CNN, our favorite news website, or in our local newspaper.

For your daily feed of good news - open your Bible.

Below are just a few examples of Good News that God has waiting for you in His Word.

- 1Corinthians 15
- Acts 2
- 1 John 5
- Ephesians 2
- John 2

Now That's Good News

God didn't promise days without pain, laughter without sorrow, nor sun without rain. But He did promise strength for the day, comfort for the tears, and light for the way.

Unknown

For God hath not given us the spirit of fear, but of power, and of love, and of a sound mind.

II Timothy 1:7

www.ingramcontent.com/pod-product-compliance
Lightning Source LLC
Chambersburg PA
CBHW060356130626
46553CB00003B/1252